CW00543734

THE NUMBER STORY

BOOK ONE

Numbers Teach Children
Their Number Names

written and illustrated by
MISS ANNA

LUMPY PUBLISHING

For my children,
David, Samuel, John and Daniel

May you love to learn
and learn to love

We are Numbers.

Numbers, wait for Zero.
ZERO is a number too!

You have seen us before.

And do we have a story

for you in store!

We are on toys,

on cards,

and on the mug shots

of crooks.

We Numbers are everywhere,

even in books!

We are important you see.

And each of us has a name,

special names they are too

like Zero, One, Two, and Three.

YET, it can be hard

to match us with the right name.

To many it is not fun

to play this matching game.

So, we worked together.

We thought of a way.

We created this STORY

for you today!

Are you ready to imagine?

Are you ready to play?

YES?

Great!

OKAY!

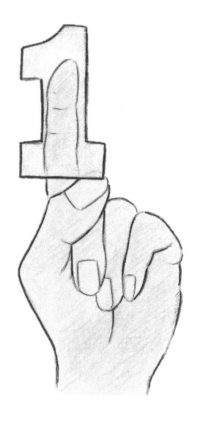

1 looks like my *one* finger.

One!

2 trails a tail.

A tail!

3 has bumps.

Bumpy!

4 carries a sail.

A sail!

five

5 is a racing track.

VROOOM!

6 curves like a snail.

A snail!

7 has a sharp angle.

Ouch!

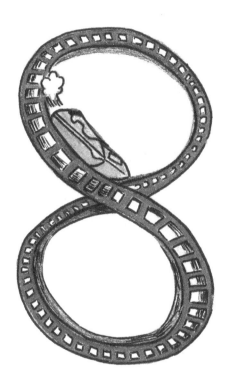

8 is rollercoaster rails.

Yippee!

is a bubble on top

of a stick.

ten

And

10 is one eye of a whale.

Wink!

How about zero?

Yeah!
How about Z E R O?

zero

Let's say that

0 is an empty pail.

It's empty!

Wow! I like that.
I like pails!

It was so much fun

to write this story!

Play with our rhymes,

and please don't you worry.

Soon, very soon,

you will remember our names.

And by and by,

you will play all our games!

So, here we go again

before we say *toodle-oo*.

And yes, we'll meet again.

This is our promise to you.

EVERYWHERE, all around you—

above, under, and through—

You will find us all waving

and smiling at you.

"Do you see us?

Over here!

YOO-HOO!"

Numbers! Numbers!
In order please!

 1 one   looks like my one finger.

 2 two   trails a tail.

 3 three   has bumps.

 4 four   carries a sail.

 5 five   is a racing track.

 6 six   curves like a snail.

Oh, our hearts jump and tingle

whenever you play our numerical jingle~

 7 seven has a sharp angle.

 8 eight is rollercoaster rails.

 9 nine is a bubble on top of a stick.

and

 10 ten is one eye of a whale.

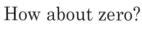

How about zero?

Let's say that

 0 zero is an empty pail.

Copyright © 2016 by Jieeun Woo
Illustrations © Jieeun Woo
Layout| Lumpy Publishing
Edited by Billy Bob Buttons

All rights reserved. No part of this book may be reproduced or transmitted in any form or by any means whatsoever, including photocopying, recording or by any information storage and retrieval system, without written permission from the publisher and/or author: missanna@missannabooks.com.

Library of Congress Control Number: 2016913243

Woo, Jieeun, author, illustrator.
    [Works. Selections]
    The number story 1 : Numbers teaches their names ;
    The number story 2 : Numbers teaches to count / written by Jieeun Woo ; illustrated by Jieeun Woo.
    58 pages, 0.75 cm
    Titles from separate title pages; works issued back-to-back and inverted (tête-bêche format).
    SUMMARY: In "Number story 1," the numbers show children a creative way to connect the numerical name to the right numerical symbol. In "Number story 2," the numbers count with children to show 1-to-1 correspondence between the numerical symbol and the act of counting.
    Audience: Ages 2-5.

    1. Numeration--Juvenile literature. 2. Number concept--Juvenile literature. 3. Numbers, Natural--Juvenile literature. 4. Counting--Juvenile literature. 5. Upside-down books. [1. Number systems. 2. Number concept. 3. Numbers, Natural. 4. Counting. 5. Upside-down books.] I. Container of (work): Woo, Jieeun. Number story 1. II. Container of (work): Woo, Jieeun. Number story 2. III. Title. IV. Title: Number story 2.

QA141.3.W66 2016   513.5
      QBI16-900037

Publisher: Lumpy Publishing
Website: www.missannabooks.com
Email: missanna@missannabooks.com

Paperback: ISBN 978-0-9962164-8-7
Hardback: ISBN 978-0-9962164-9-4

Printed in the U.S.A.   2 0 10 6 1 5 2 0

Author Bio

Miss Anna ✿

Let us write.

Let us draw.

Let us create for all.

Learning should be fun.

The half-steps have begun.

Oh, to see them smile, lil' ones big and small.

- Miss Anna

MISS ANNA is a mother of four. A writing teacher by training, she enjoys writing educational stories that provide an understanding of foundational concepts, numbers being one of them. She writes on behalf of the Numbers (which she attests are not a bore at all), and she wishes all children to grow up loving them, their peculiar shapes and all. Oh, the stories that they do tell!

THE NUMBER STORY 1 & 2

Numbers Teach Children Their Number Names

Numbers Count with Children
ISBN: (softcover) 978-0-996216-48-7
ISBN: (hardcover) 978-0-996216-49-4

THE NUMBER STORY 3 & 4

Numbers Introduce Eleven, Twelve, and the Teens

Numbers Teach Children Their Ordinal Names
ISBN: (softcover) 978-1-945977-01-5
ISBN: (hardcover) 978-1-945977-10-7

THE NUMBER STORY 5 & 6

Around the World with Numbers 0-99

The Invisible Chairs of Numberland
ISBN: (softcover) 978-1-945977-06-0
ISBN: (hardcover) 978-1-949320-31-2

THE NUMBER STORY 7 & 8

Dr. Zee's Museum of Once Upon A Time

Dr. Zee Gets a Hand to Tell Time
ISBN: (softcover) 978-1-949320-40-4
ISBN: (hardcover) 978-1-949320-41-1

Make numbers come alive

with the award-winning

THE NUMBER STORY!

An inspirational, clever, and fun way
of helping children enjoy learning about numbers.

THE NUMBER STORY 1 (Small Book Version)
has been translated into over 100 languages!

MP3

You can sing-a-long with the Numbers as well.
Lookf for *Miss Anna Number Story*
in your favorite music platform.

You can count with Numbers

EVERYDAY!

So, do call on us

A N Y T I M E !

To remember our names,

use our rhymes.

And come count with us.

It is a game you can play.

Counting is fun

when you count with us,

Numerical buddies

that you can trust.

One looks like
my *one* finger!

Two trails
a tail!

We will help you count

just about EVERYTHING,

From socks, to dolls,

to beads on a string.

Let's count again!

7 seven **Puzzles**
Puzzle Pieces

8 eight **Pins**
Safety Pins

Trumpets

10 ten **Tins**

And

0 zero Zins

Numbers! Numbers!

1 one   Fire Truck

2 two   Twins

3 three   Baseballs

4 four   Bins

5 five   Feathers

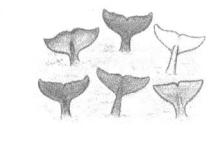

6 six   Fins

Tail Fins/Caudal Fins

ZINS?

We know.

Zins is not a word.

It is nothing, *zilch*, *zip*!

We just wanted to see you grin.

And 0 Zins

Zins

6 Trumpets

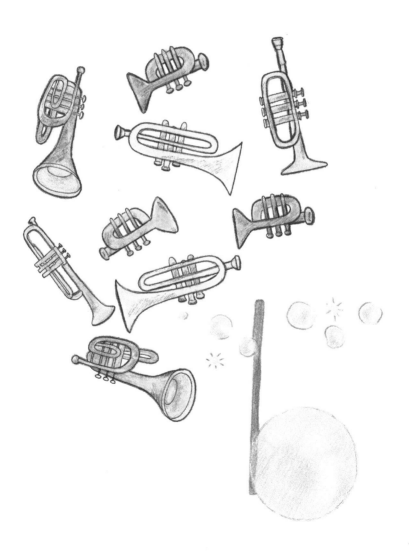

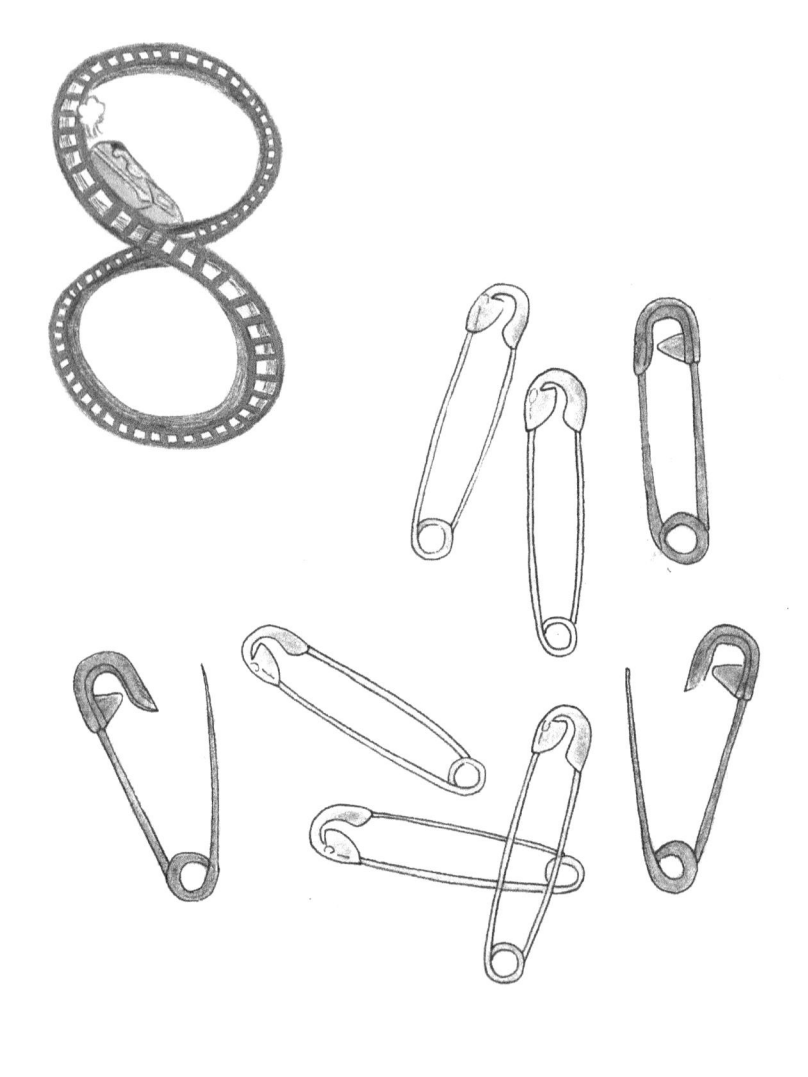

8 Pins
(Safety Pins)

7

Puzzles
(Puzzle Pieces)

6 Fins
(Tail Fins/Caudal Fins)

Fluke is another word for a whale's tail fin.

5

5 Feathers

4 Bins

3 Baseballs

 Twins

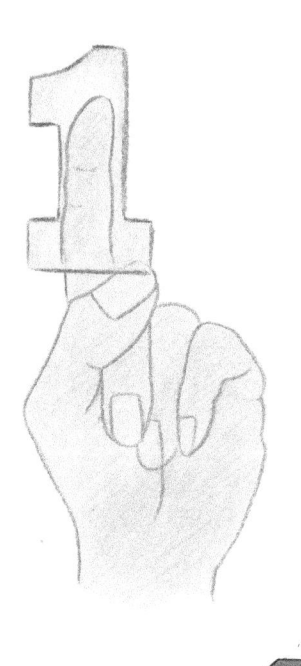

1 Fire Truck

Let's start the game!

YAY! Whoopee!

Come count with us –

one, two, three ~

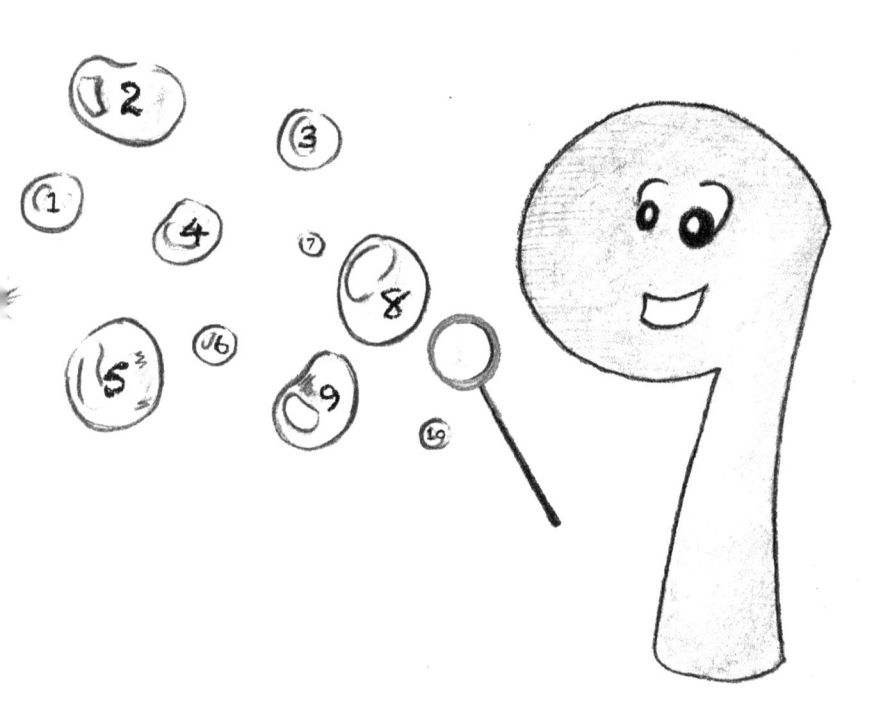

And counting is a game

that is fun, fun, fun!

We love to play games.

We love to have fun!

We are Numbers,

your friends evermore.

Let's play a game

that all Numbers adore!

THE
NUMBER
STORY

BOOK TWO

Numbers Count with Children

written and illustrated by

M I S S   A N N A

LP LUMPY PUBLISHING

Lightning Source UK Ltd.
Milton Keynes UK
UKHW020337131121
393861UK00001B/16